I Am Not I

By Louise Machen

Editor: Matthew M. C. Smith
www.blackboughpoetry.com
Twitter/X: @blackboughpoems
Insta: @blackboughpoetry
FB: BlackBoughpoetry
Also on Bluesky

Author: Louise Machen
Website: www.louisemachen.com
Twitter/ X: @louloumach
Insta: @louloumachpoetry
Bluesky: louloumach@bluesky.social

Published by Black Bough Poetry in 2025.
Copyright © 2025

LEGAL NOTICE The right of Matthew M. C. Smith to be identified as the editor of this work has been asserted in accordance with the Copyright, Designs and Patents Act 1988.

All rights reserved. No part of this book may be reproduced, stored in a retrieval system, or transmitted in any form, or by any means; electronic, mechanical, photocopying, without prior permission from the author and editor. However, short extracts may be quoted on social media.

Cover painting: *The Emperor's New Clothes* by Dylan Lisle

Dedication

For my dad, his patience and his kindness.

Acknowledgements

Sincerest thanks to Matthew M.C. Smith for his encouragement, time and care in editing this collection.

To the editors of journals who have published my work, to those who have offered me a place on their stage to share my words and to the poets and readers who have extended their kindness – thank you.

To Dylan, for the use of his wonderful artwork and for providing me with the physical and emotional space to complete this collection – thank you. I appreciate you so much.

To Hope, my daughter, who has listened to draft after draft, year upon year – you embody your name so beautifully. Thank you for your unwavering support.

Advanced Testimonies

"'I sing the world/ to kill this knowing' affirms the first speaker in Louise Machen's collection. The musical language that follows is urgent. It confronts a dark backdrop through crafted, sensuous imagery, daring the reader to 'Wade in, take the risk.'"

John McCullough, author of *Panic Response*

"Louise Machen both creates and explores her own literary tradition in her debut collection, *I Am Not Light*. Through dizzying line-breaks and a complex control of speed, Machen explores loss and living amidst a raw and wild landscape. The speaker of her poems is multiple, part ghost in absence, and yet, we find her sitting next to us on the bus. To balance such distance with the personal is a complex feat which Machen masters. To be both grounded and heartbroken simultaneously makes this one of the most exciting contemporary poets I have read."

Wendy Allen, author of *Portrait in Mustard*

"It is a fine day when a writer is so staggered that she is lost for words and this, after reading *I Am Not Light*, is the joyous position I find myself in now. Machen's work is more than words; there is a drive and dynamism in her poetry that can only be felt – mysterious intimations that tug quietly at the throat, prickle the eyes, clutch at the heart. She is, to borrow her own perfect term, edgeless, as she pays homage to the rich lyricism of her poetic ancestors – Plath in particular comes to mind – while carving her own brilliant future, where her impeccable poetic voice sings as a timeless, boundless marvel."

Briony Collins, author of *Blame it on Me*

"Many of Louise Machen's poems in *I Am Not Light* seek out and describe shorelines and borders, and those moments when change happens, or is wished for: these poems know 'impossible depths / and hope of a handhold' as she puts it in 'In Pursuit of Edges'. But this book is alert too to the kind of grace that is found in poems like 'Pebbles and Bricks', when the speaker can declare, 'I am light in your hands'. And in the middle of these poems of becoming is a set of affecting family poems describing a childhood which will, I am sure, be remembered by everyone who reads them."

John McAuliffe, University of Manchester's Centre for New Writing, author of *Next Door*

"If poetry is both the reader and writer making sense of the world, then this collection by Louise Machen seeks to achieve this on an elemental level. Immersed in the turbulence of nature; its raging seas, orange moons and secret gardens, the author takes a hand full of each and sculpts something that gives a shared understanding of all the facets of being alive that are sometimes so difficult to hold. There is grief, loss, love, and yet a feeling of familiarity. It is in this magic that Machen manages to speak to the deepest parts of our subconsciousness, and in doing so inadvertently makes us feel more alive"

Stuart McPherson, author of *End Ceremonies*

Foreword

It's a privilege to publish Manchester poet, Louise Machen, with her debut poetry collection, *I Am Not Light*, a coup for Black Bough Poetry. Louise is a phenomenal writer, one who is quite uniquely able to tap into the most troubled emotional undercurrents of life with immense word power, an engaging, full-throttle poetics displaying great conviction and soul. There's something simultaneously heartbreaking and moving about lines like these:

I sing to the world to kill this knowing ('Family Tree')

Failed by prayer,
she tore the heads from devils ('The Abbess')

Do not drown me now
in their loneliness. ('In Need of a Closer Shore')

At last, my heart is full ('Openhanded')

Machen allows us to look at the highs and lows of our own lives in the most modern idiom, without affectation or pretension. This collection, with its dramatic intensity, burns with betrayal, pulses with love, and fights with grief at every turn, half-revealing painful truths. The poems dealing with personal pilgrimage to the ocean's edge really take the reader and listener there – to a sense of true escape and freedom from despair.

I hope you enjoy and are moved by this work. Please rate, review, rave about it. Why not gift it?

I'd like to thank all of the writers who gave testimonies and to the supreme artistic talent of Dylan Lisle. One of the best poetry covers ever? You decide!

Matthew M. C. Smith

About the Author

Louise Machen is a Mancunian poet and educator. She holds a BA in English Literature from the University of Manchester and an MA in Creative Writing from The Centre for New Writing at the same institution.

Her work has been widely published in various journals and magazines including *The Poetry Bus* (nominated for The Forward Prize, Single Poem), *Dreich*, *Acropolis Journal*, *Black Bough Poetry*, *The Morning Star* and *Cape Magazine*. Louise has been a featured poet at *East Ridge Review* with a poem nominated for the Pushcart Prize; she has also had two poems nominated for Best of the Net.

Her collaborative pamphlet, 'The Words of Others are All We Have', published by *Hedgehog Poetry*, was staged at Manchester Fringe Festival in Summer 2024 with her co-author J. Daniel West where critics described it as, "thought provoking, gritty and evocative."

A teacher of literature for over a decade, she is also regular speaker at poetry events across the city of Manchester and beyond. She has headlined at Band on the Wall for Verbose, The Golden Lion, BBC Radio Manchester, Rhyming Words and TME English Icons, among many others.

Artist biography – Dylan Lisle

Born in 1978 in Darlington, Durham, Dylan Lisle studied Fine Art at Gray's School of Art in Aberdeen, Scotland. Lisle has strong connections with the Scottish art community having painted from studios in both Edinburgh and Aberdeen. Now based in Manchester, he continues to paint at 1853 Studios in Oldham, Greater Manchester.

Lisle's style of work stems from an appreciation of the dark, moody and striking images found in Baroque and Classical art. The strong chiaroscuro lighting of Caravaggio and the tactile quality of Titian's drapery are of great influence. Lisle borrows elements of these styles and marries them with unusual, challenging poses and compositions more reminiscent of 20th Century work. Website: www.dylanlisle.com

About the editor

Matthew M. C. Smith is a writer from Swansea. He has two chapbooks, 'Origin: 21 Poems' and 'Paviland: Ice and Fire' and a full collection, *The Keeper of Aeons*. Matthew edits Black Bough Poetry, the Silver Branch project and runs online platform TopTweetTuesday. He has guest edited for other presses and reviewed for *Poetry Wales* and *London Grip*. He is campaigning for the return of the Red Lady of Paviland, the body of an Ice Age Hunter found in a Gower cave, back to Swansea from Oxford, where it has been for the past 202 years.

I Am Not Light

I. Into the Darkness   2

Family Tree	4
The Abbess	5
The Unforgiven	6
Shore-Bound	7
In Need of a Closer Shore	8
Exposure	9
Defunct Radio Station on a Cliff Edge	10
The Tenth Muse	11
Take Me Out to Sea	12
In Pursuit of Edges	13
Lines in the Sand	14
Dunskey Castle at Daybreak	15
The Cave of Uchtrie Macken	16
The Crab	17
Lunation	18
Dawning	19
Amazonite	21
Vapours	22
And then, We Never Spoke Again	23
Moss	24
Dirt	25
I Am Not Light	26

II. Origins of Darkness   28

April   30
1989   31
The Queen of Sheba   32
The Playground   33
Damsonflies   34
Keepsake   35
A Disremembering   36
I Stand Outside Your House and Try to Remember   38
House Clearance   39
Strawberries   40
Splinters   41
A Burnt Child Dreads the Fire   42
Familial Obligation   43
An Involuntary Truth   44
On Sundays   45
Dreaming   46
Deathbed   47
People Disappear   48
Words Never Spoken   49
Unspeakable Things   51
Grief Therapist   52
Truth-Telling   53

III. Into the Light   54

Becoming an Arborist   56
Clearing the Wall Without Permission   57
Violets   58
Penelope and Odysseus   59
Cartographer   60
The Old Master   61
El Corazon   62
Pebbles and Bricks   63
Nightingale   64
Openhanded   65

Recommended reading   68
Bonus Poems   70

"There is no sun without shadow and it is essential to know the night." Albert Camus

I

Into the Darkness

Family Tree

I belong to the branches,
but not the roots;
to the scent of balsam,
to heart-shaped leaves –
my yellow-green catkins
symbiotic with the wind:
visible, sunlit.

I belong to the branches,
but not the roots;
wound together, burrowing
to reach the Lethe in hope
of forgetting, of reincarnation –
I sing to the world
to kill this knowing.

The Abbess

after St Hilda

Seabirds genuflect, dipping their grace
towards the golden grasses
of a sainted serpent-slayer.

Failed by prayer,
she tore the heads from devils
to create sanctuary
for honest words.

A trick of the light allows you
to see her in that glorified state –
I sit with ammonites,
beneath the holy moon,
praying to be uncoiled from stone.

The Unforgiven

      lie behind closed doors,
ears burning, bound in spiky heat
and the company of cold shoulders.

      Contrite smiles stretch from ear to ear
stapled in place by pretence of contentment –
hope for acceptance – severed tongues upon the offertory plate.

      Watch me hold my breath as though the rot
of unforgiven sin oozes from my open mouth,
aging my gait, thickening my skin.

      I observe everything: senses fine-tuned in limbo
to the critics' tone of voice, to the pitch that precedes
the raking of scabs into scars – the removal of ours.

      When acts of contrition are no longer currency,
the larvae of guilt festers, a myiasis of remorse
thrashing in response to spoon-fed shame,

      washed down with the last brew from the pot –
bitter, every drop. Pustules of regret animate:
unable to heal, they burst from oppressed space,

      spilling onto carpets of broken eggshell,
pupating into indifference. The unforgiven are dangerous
people; what have they to lose?

Shore-Bound

Circling sea birds cry:
you've been shore-bound in this life –
wade in, take the risk.

In Need of a Closer Shore

After the MV Princess Victoria Memorial - Portpatrick

Granite-bolted above my wind-torn head,
her greenish hands hang from iron history
above a sharp and steely sea –
fingers splayed and clinging
like a mother's desperation
to recover the awe of infancy.

Flogged by the air, I edge broadside
and the picture becomes whole
where pasts erode like sea stacks
falling in on themselves –
a short crossing, a solitary shift
from which returning will always mark disaster.

Gusts form abrasions like a scolding
from her matriarchal tongue,
whipping this child who is too close to the abyss –
a daughter distracted, peeling feet from algae,
unwilling to let go of her fractured vessel,
as water floods the deck of attrition
sluicing legs of broken timber.
Do not drown me now
in their loneliness.

Exposure

Pincered by black rocks of the headland,
an anchor, chain-links the shape of praying hands,
is pummelled by northern tides –
the illusion of solidity burnished with an umber crust.
Its fixings are worn away; its friable edges decay
with each salt breath – weathered and sunblasted,
iron heart on fire, where briny air
turns my skin a reddish hue.

Rust-flecked, it eats away at itself,
leaning from the edge, anticipating collapse –
we are tethered by gravity alone.

A Defunct Radio Station on a Cliff Edge

is shuttered and blockaded
by grey uniformity.

Gorse reflects in monochrome
against the steely grates
belonging to this hotch-potch
of squat and lean structures –
not a symbol of fertility,
but navigation lights
dotted along the coastline
like candles at Lourdes
praying for abandoned voices.

This coastal radio dispatch
has been replaced with automation
and the distress calls of gulls
riding harsh winds –
a thin light presses me back
into the last century,
willing me to alert the lifeboats,
to tear down yellow triangles
and their exclamations,
driving me beyond the gates
to broadcast myself across the waves.

The Tenth Muse

After 'Sappho' by Charles Auguste Mengin

Linen of the blackest gossamer barely covers
her perfection: moonlit and songless,
veil and hair billow into the night.
She turns her back to the pearly light
that lies along the horizon
and becomes the funereal surf.

From her right hand,
the hollow body of a lyre hangs,
mute and paled by introspection –
the salt-air fails to strike a melody.
She is empty and undaunted
by dangers of the cliff edge
where seabirds sail their silhouettes
among restless waves and a starless sky.
Veins of gold light paths to sleep-starved eyes,
staring down on bare-footed translations of chaos.

You burn me, she says, as men read themselves
into the fragments of a woman in the blackness,
all alone.

Take Me Out to Sea

Take me out to sea.
Leave me there –
salt water in my eyes
and songs in my ears.

Carry me into the waves.
Let me go
where I can't touch the floor,
but embrace the depths as you

submerge me,
one hand on my head –
a baptism
into the planetary core.

Push me further away
from your shore.
I will asphyxiate on algae
and promises.

Allow me to sink.

Allow me to sink.

Tell me there will be no rescue.

In Pursuit of Edges

She is edgeless a body of water
thick with salinity red sea buoyancy
washing me toward the horizon
swallowing my inarticulate
prayer for immersion.

Saltwater tongues sing electric
transmissions across the membrane
of want my blazing
blue-fire extremities
track her in reflections

of trailing stars, sailing
this topography no ships, no cannons
just tidal forces impossible depths
and hope of a handhold.

Lines in the Sand

                weave across the shoreline –
flood-formed ripples, ridges and runnels,
      trace the edge of being

      where rill marks from the falling tide are laced
along my crooked spine, the way snakes
      will vacillate to find their way back to belonging.

      This makeshift stream gives way to the shadow
of a forest between seaweed and rock –
      delicate branches splayed like oil in puddles
feathering the land.

      Tomorrow, these contours will be gone –
drowned by the swell. What remains will soak into the earth
      or drag itself towards the sea,
leaving lines in the sand that mean nothing.

Dunskey Castle at Daybreak

Crows empty from ancient brick:
a cyclone of shadow carving salt air
and a sky opaque with longing.

I hear only their wings and the waves
as I howl a mimicry of a memory –
song of a long-forgotten prisoner

masked by squalls, wrapping this damp hair
around my face. I decorate myself in black
feathers, wanting it to mean more than this.

The Cave of Uchtrie Macken

It's not yet the first day of May
and I bring my inner child
to cleanse beneath the spring
that oils the rock at Port Mora.

A glassy blackness underfoot
mirrors our portal to Eternia –
cloaked in flowerless gorse,
witness to the seals of Sandeel bay.

Here, my strangeness bores
into the landscape
and our likeness reverberates
in the cave's rebarbative façade.

She holds me in contempt
beneath this healing cascade
and we spill into the sky –
a murmuration of regret.

The Crab

a found poem

I realise now it was dead:
belly-up and pale,
yellowing like skirting boards in old houses

its little gut caged
like the mandible of an arthropod –
aesthetic in its emptiness,

vulnerable to sea birds
and the ebb of a negligent tide,
legs melting into rock.

Yesterday, I saw it
flaxen and alive on the face
of the moon

and today in your palm,
where still my petrified hesitance
abandons the possibility of a life.

Lunation

The orange moon is full with staying
– rusting lantern of the morning,

shepherding this new-found obscurity
and another year of limited welcome.

Furze lines the path: a gilded barrier
against an enormity of sea and sky –

striding azurite flecked with a fishing boat,
dipping into the horizon like an idea flickering

beyond small epiphanies taking flight.
I remain unseen watching the tiny craft

on the edge of the ocean, searching for its catch,
as I try to photograph the moon –

her light stretching into brush strokes;
warping her majesty like gold in the fire.

Dawning

I

Today's pilgrimage leads to the clifftop –
a steep ascent of metamorphic rock
and troughs ground into the face of the earth.
Flanked by ailing grass,
legs thick with fatigue
angle the crest of the track,
only pausing to pull life into lungs
marooned by thin air.

II

Waves under crags smite the edge of solace
as tiptoes trip on broken edges
of time-worn sandstone,
following this well-trodden descent,
where the sea swamps the land
and wind-wolves gorge themselves
on this empty cove.

III

White veins of saltwater baptise flat stones –
gifting seaweed to the earth
then drawing it back
into bubbles breathing foam along slick sand:
a veil of renewal embroidering the shore,
whispering its sacrament of reconciliation,
offering to slough away the ashen promises of this world.

IV

I rest in the brackish groundswell
accompanied by driftwood and pebbles –
sunken and shining,
speckled like the misplaced eggs of a mistle thrush,
awaiting mutation in the cold light.
Others, grey with pink and silver ripples,
are shaped by their perilous journey,
white halo tips marbled to perfection,
like my skin in these cold tides of sanctum,
like the day that has begun again.

Amazonite

In legend, this treasure in my palm would line boss-shields
of warrior queens – crescent-shaped peltas of protection,
guarding the daughters of Ares, flecked and streaked
with streams of a paler shade.

Potassium feldspar veins, enriched by the sun, are said
to mend, to turn those small deaths into origins of pride,
to sweep the dirt of a homeless mind into a vitrified lustre –
one polished of past injuries and the scuffs of old beliefs.

This stone of truth, recovered from pharaohs' tombs,
is a talisman for the afterlife, alongside tablets of amazonite,
cut with The Book of the Dead, singing:
I am the shelter of every god.

And every god rests in my hand, reciting their funerary rites
through impressions of lunar light,
as I sit in my ordinariness – awash in anonymity
as though we are both living things.

Vapours

Waves explode like memory
raging to revive buried episodes,
their white fingers clawing at the synapse
of rocks nestled by the shoreline.
They scour at surety,
reshaping with each surge,
curling into themselves like seahorses –
a salty quickening of corrosion,
sounding a morning hymnal,
lashing the seafoam of loss.

And Then, We Never Spoke Again

like a cliff collapsed –
rocks retiring into the sea
after a life of holding:

a dehydrated plateau
stretching years of distance,
decorated with the scabs
of a motherless silence.

Pointless trying to revive
the greenish shoots beneath,
suffocating in the broken earth –

too much work for so little,
for just a smile,
for just *I love you.*

Moss

My head is cradled by stone
as I am remade in part of a wood
the sun never sees.

The scent of rot breathes
beneath Tamarisk moss,
rising from green-black stems,

whispering honesties into hair
that winds into the ground,
anchoring me to the soil,

burrowing into caverns beneath:
a network of blooming intricacies
where I become moss,

mending what can't be seen,
feeding the hum of cold earth,
its flora filling my veins –

cocooned and concealed,
awaiting my timely release.

Dirt

This dirt on my knees is ingrained
in the creases of my skin.
You don't see it? Look closely.
It was ground in
behind those child-like eyes

where black capillaries spray a winter sky.
Hair on damp earth – mossy and paralysed.
Fed-upon. Dirt-covered. Wordless. Still.

See, if I were to peel away the years,
exhuming soil horizons,
layers of gritty filth would spill
like marbles uncontained;
buried in nonchalance,
the colour of memory fades.

Don't let my blue lips bother you,
at times I forget to breathe –
but these burrowing insects,
beneath the encasement,
remind me they are still alive
in their sempiternal state.

Sorry, I'll get dressed
and put this all away.

I Am Not Light

I am not light-fast. I fade at the edges –
sun-bleached like memory disputed by time.
Life leaches brilliance from fibres
of urgency – bright ochre flames,
doused in gin and midnight.

I claim these thinning gowns
and wear them crowned in gold;
there is no daylight without erasure.
And though sunshine has worn me away,
I welcome its heat on my face,

but only on occasion –
a lucid illumination of age.
Forgive me, I am not light,
but a palette of colour-washed darkness
trying to preserve what little I have left.

II

Origins of Darkness

April

I was born on a Monday:
appearing prematurely at one in the morning –
too much haemoglobin and a finger-hold
on the thread of life's intention.

The hummingbird in my chest
followed us to our red-brick terraced house –
black door in a mill town,
home to silk-cloth pioneers
and the fuchsia that flowers in April.

While I mended, you smoked Bensons,
prepping bottles for the night feed
and the expectations of my tiny, furrowed brow.

Now, we sit – same house, different faces.
The garden needs weeding,
as colours flower and decay,
knowing, soon enough, this house
will be too small for the both of us.

1989

It was the year we trafficked frogspawn
from the pond beside the bookies.

We were mirrors of each other:
Clockhouse labels, Opal Fruits,
laburnum flowers in our hair,
garden-hopping with our spoils
stashed in a cracked fish tank.

And there they sat —
watching us from behind the shed window
in their crystalline jam, turning.

Some began to bud
until spring warmed up
and they were cooked in the sunlight.

The Queen of Sheba

I push my fingers through ratted hair
waiting for the bus to change drivers.
The sickly smell of July teases my hangover
as winged ants on their nuptial flight
smash into stationary windows.

I'm late, but the back yard looks the same –
a clean view to the kitchen, echoes of
Who do you think you are?
peering through the glass,
flavoured like tinned oranges
and Carnation milk.

My stomach turns with tequila and the ache
of delinquency. I reach back to pluck out
futile wings, hoping for an uneventful
entrance, knowing later, we'll pretend
she was crying over onions.

The Playground

All that remains is a wall –
witness to coarse language we'd kick
around on summer afternoons:
pretending to know what we'd said,
pretending we knew who we were.

I lean into a vague familiarity
encroached upon by housing I don't recognise.
Weeds grow in memories of worn hopscotch,
how we'd spend our after-schools:
drinking Tizer, playing truth or dare,
adults desperate to tell us unimportant things.

Clouds part purposefully leaving
truths in their trails –
the revelation of who we are when faced
with swings lacking seats.
The dare is in the living despite
what we've been left with, or without.

Eyes closed; I sink between gaps in the brick –
trying to forget where I came from.

Damsonflies

I have gone out alone,
hunting for *damsonflies*,
blue like the jam I stirred
into rice pudding when I was eight:
chipped tooth and home-cut fringe.

The day you leant over the canal edge,
they were resting on the reeds –
an iridescent eye
on you
as we picked the fern
mum still grows in her garden.

Flying in tandem,
you'd say how they got their blue:
Babylonian indigo plants,
Middle Eastern fairies,
lapis lazuli paintbrushes
and a reckless dragonfly falling
into a pool of goblin blood.

I'd pretend to forget,
you'd tell me again.
I can still feel the sugar on my teeth
from the sarsaparilla tablets we'd share.

Coming back,
I watch her sleep, eyes half open,
as if she doesn't want to miss a thing,
as if she's waiting
for *damsonflies*.

Keepsake

Rosary beads rest
in a plain black box,
last stirred by your pleas
a lifetime ago.

Mahogany pearls
flash amber in the light
when they run through my hands
like time with you.

The arbiter of sin, of penance,
of *Hail Marys* and *Our Fathers* –
I still stumble on *forgive us our trespasses*
hoping for comfort in my confessions.

Maybe if God's house had been
decorated in brick wallpaper,
had served ginger ale in small glasses,
I'd have been more inclined to sit and listen.

If each globe of prayer was cast
with one of your stories,
each bead-cap linked to another
in narrative glory,
perhaps I'd read them a little more often.

I'd say I was sorry I never followed
your lead, never took your advice,
or believed in your idea of consequence,
but I'm not. I bathe in my aftermath daily.

A Disremembering

A corner of the evening set aside,
he sits at the kitchen table –
sharpening pencils with a flick knife,
sipping Guinness from a mug.

Slices of rusted sky reflect from the oil cloth,
casting shadows on his jawline
as he glowers through the distance
at his skinny dog.

There's a sad grace to his action,
the way he strips the wood from the lead,
away from the body, with stiff precision
the same way he would strip skin
from flesh, flesh from bone:
prayerful and rapt.

A certain holiness clings
to his tattered doilies and cracked china –
placemats he's never used
kept for company he doesn't need.

Lists of errands,
names and pages from his phone book
are tacked onto woodchip
waiting for recognition,
for recollection, for deliverance.

Blow heaters filch the air –
the dog's hoarse panting grates
at his sanity until it echoes
in the thump of the pulse in his mind

and all he recalls is 1942
and clarity, and clarity, and clarity.

He doesn't notice me
until sometime after I've arrived.
Misremembering my name,
he points at the pencils,
opens a window and walks away.

I Stand Outside Your House and Try to Remember

His Singapore shadow spills from a green door,
over red brick coping stones, into the quiet road
where I approach the past of a Northern lad
who barked in Japanese while children slept.

My photographs are other people's memories
of this cobbled street, when I fit into the crook
of his arm, held by the scarred palms
he would press down into the window ledge –

thick-framed glasses gazing at the garage,
its awnings red and white, painted like half
a rising sun. *It's in his blood*, she'd say,
like tattoos made with the pin of his Pacific Star,

Sunday naptime, dripping butties, hands in pockets,
pints of bitter bought with her housekeeping money,
hateful voices, double Dutch and no rice pudding.
His presence lingers like the scent

of other people's freshly washed belongings in the sun –
this place he would fire all his guns at once,
exacting obedience with his dog-eared prayer book
lined with notes of things he wouldn't talk about.

A voyeur and collector of third-hand stories,
I join the magpies with their military salute
to collapsible and sunless memories –
somewhere lies an elegy, but not here.

House Clearance

Photographs on the window-ledge
are sun-bleached and obscured
by months of dust.

I create a furrow with my finger,
potted palms tied with red ribbon
perch on your shoulders –
shirt sleeves rolled to your elbows,
a cig behind your ear.

Our Lady watches from where woodchip meets lino
as nicotine-stained nets are taken down
and an unreturned volume of Hilaire Belloc
gets stacked between toothpicks
and artificial flowers.

Purple kings and their mounted men
rode through here a long time ago –
before the roundness of your cheeks
was excavated by late nights and early mornings,
before I realised the silver of your hair
had a yellowish hue.

There are no rooms on the other side
of this wall, just space.
I am the dirty rascal
and this castle has no king,
just a half-story
where hoardings and habits are undone.

Strawberries

The strawberry plants that flowered in spring
have been wiped out in this morning's storm

along with the garden fence and the tiny
cloche they were housed in.

I can't help thinking they'll be nothing for breakfast
and I don't want to go home.

This coffee tastes cheap and the concern
of strangers is unsettling.

I have my clothing in a sealed bag, but no reply
to my messages. They tell me I'm free to leave

when all I'm left with are bloodstained jeans
and this lonely bus ride.

Splinters

The speakers in my poems are splinters
of mirrored glass – spears of memory
shot forth like saboteurs
from shattered panes of past.
They intrude into present flesh,
carving tongues from echoes of old disasters –
shadows in a burning sun.

A Burnt Child Dreads the Fire

I dare to get out of bed each day,
wash my face in troubled waters,
rough flannel, tender cheeks
– skin aflame from the fingertips
of yesterday's reluctant ownership.

I keep my breathing shallow,
beneath a square of sodden cotton,
as though this room is smoke-filled
– made safe by makeshift blindfolds
and a thin but bolted door.

I souse the canvas of my flesh,
hot water pooled in porcelain,
the slop and slough echoes
– a rhythmic meditation
made orange in the dawning light.

I recite the rules by rote
by heart, by practise, practise, practise
by trial and by error, so quietly
the hum of my voice is a vaporous elegy
to rebellion: a softly spoken slander.

I have been taught the right way
and my way are not always the same.
I pat the notes of my learning dry
– water drains away. There is breakfast
to be made with clean hands for glass smiles.

Familial Obligation

Treading time like water,
shallow courtesy seeps from my visit
like the lethargy of life
seeps from her pores:
desperate to escape
like a child at Mass on Sunday.

Hymns aren't mimed here,
nor are they softly sung,
this is purgatory for us:
tea, toast and trite conversation.

I am indifferent to her agony,
an audience of apathy among the chintz
and fatigue. My pity is balanced
between basket-loads of bedsheets
and the wiping of rheum from paper skin.

Silence ferments, playing host
to my venial sins and I pray
for the moment we both slip away.

An Involuntary Truth

                        rests in a chair,
fitting neatly into its padded palm,
sickness shrouded in her tasselled pall,
hiding a tongue that has lost its way
around ordinary words.

She searches for them with the voice
of a small child – eyes wide like the saucers
in which we'd spill our tea to avoid sipping
from a hot cup.

Errors in this game of hangman
ignite the accelerant of my sweat,
trailing my arm, crossing my neck –
a head on fire,
a mouth ablaze,
burning like a devil in prayer.

Rebel Glow

On Sundays, I stand motionless beneath the raging sun,
breathless and disowned, pierced with heat and sorrow,
listening for the comfort of alone or maybe someone

translating silence into peace. Muting mind-bound reruns,
I wash my sins in fire where others will not follow.
On Sundays, I stand motionless beneath the raging sun;

the lies I tell myself wear thin; my tongue gets numb
from reciting promises, fingers crossed, meaning hollowed,
listening for the comfort of alone or maybe someone

that sounds like yesterday, sounds like absolution, like love
not contingent on perfection. I can only be things I know.
On Sundays, I stand motionless beneath the raging sun:

aflame with disillusion, bloodied with this honest song.
My faults rescind your judgement; I am kindled by this rebel
glow, listening for the comfort of alone or maybe someone

with light footsteps and a chorus that can be spun
into an embrace that illumes my errant shadow.
On Sundays I stand motionless beneath the raging sun,
listening for the comfort of alone or maybe someone.

Dreaming

                    with spiders in my mouth.
A mass of spindly legs,
like wax-covered cotton threads,
hunting sentences to swathe in silk
and spin into loose and messy webs.

They breed – a siege on epiglottal articulation
reaping line upon line –
as these clumsy fingers struggle to pincer
this thistledown we'd wish on as children.

Eyes open, I grasp at hordes of tiny human skulls
painting my soft palate with sepia privacies,
emerging with slivers of truth

from nights filled with false awakenings
and the corners of a house
that does not belong to me.

Deathbed

Reams of heavy silk
burst from my throat
smothering attempts
to articulate affection
in this fallow place.

I reach for her
and my fingers turn to ribbons,
their doubt-cut dovetails
mauling silent air.

Threads turn in on themselves
and flightless honesties return
to a heart of white moths –
a cloud of impotent wings
dusted with the dread of loss.

People Disappear

                        not like in the movies
with dramatic sirens and searches and confusion.

Quietly. They leave.

Now, there's no need to buy two kinds of milk,
but your absent-mindedness forgets.
Until you see someone who can't be them,
and the certainty of their vanishing drags memory,
like a marauder, kicking and screaming into the dairy aisle –
belting out its silent tantrum beneath strip-lights
and strangers and into a basket empty of milk,
but brimming with the sour taste of absence.

Words Never Spoken

                    are sacrificed to the fire
                    one by one.

Peeled from the throats
of tardy penitents,

                    each one burns differently
                    in their makeshift pyre.

Copper-covered clavicles,
bruised with retching,

                    flush green from flames,
                    their poisoned lexes

giving way to briny remorse,
igniting sooty-yellow sparks

                    to blind their confessors
                    with the brightness of their folly.

Old hurts hauled through coals
hit heat and flare like bouts of rage

                    yielding to scarlet shadows,
                    dancing in drowned irises,

rubied with resentment
that will never be remedied.

                    The syntax of torment reflects
                    the lavender of their pallor,

surrendering to calcified affections,
thick with atrophy,

                      resistant to resurrection,
                      crying out an orange blaze –

until only regret remains
in remnants of ash.

Unspeakable Things

Crows rake the sky –
their guttural serenade to lost summers
flying overhead.

Clouds heave across the leaden
afternoon, becoming ripe
in her absence,
pregnant with an autumnal August,
like my mouth
with these unspeakable things.

Grief Therapist

Put hemlock in the teapot.
Place fire beneath to expedite
the pollution of parasol clusters:
tuberous roots, thickened like hearts
after deceit – thriving in damp spots
left by tears.

Cut a cross-section of crushed odours
from memory and muscle.
Mimic humanity with tea in small glasses.
Drink from the pot
because water is scarce,
because your body is a drought
begging to be quenched
by the poisons we feed ourselves.

Truth-Telling

A crow opens its beak
and my words come out –
drawn from her throat
like lost hair from a drain.

Syllables of burnt sugar
stick like shadows
to the bill of my envoi –
tar-covered vitriol
rankled by inertia,
hardened in the winter air.

Her guiro purge forces flight –
shedding my darkness
like an almost-black dahlia
beneath the honest sun.

III

Into the Light

Becoming an Arborist

The shedding of sticks is a symptom:
dull starburst of cankers in the brain
driving decay to the extremity of existence.

When leaves have fallen, trunk and limbs hewed,
a cyclical miracle occurs deep in the earth.
The pallbearers of new life feed the soil –
an heirloom of shelter persisting where roots
have sprawled beyond their branches –
a posthumous mothering of nutrients and knowledge.

Above ground, this language of legacy leaks
through thread-like hypha – footings of hope
thriving in death on a diet of necessary rot
where split bark is trimmed and broken down
to fuel residual growth.

In spring, the constancy of tyrian blooms
will cluster around this base of dead wood –
only then, will I remove my gardening robes
and let the bluebells breathe me in.

Clearing the Wall Without Permission

Greenery, on the cusp of blossoming,
ripped from its nest of clay,
burns in an old wheelbarrow,
burns so darkly, the bricks behind
move as if to Orpheus' song –
dirge of a magical death.

The starkness of a boundary line,
austere in its emptiness,
whispers short days into thick air
standing beneath perpetual dusk,
dragging laments from the open throat
of a force-fed fire eater.

Now, in April, nature returns.
Lilac waves crossing chipped mortar –
a world of life and light
finding its way from grief.
I look back to share this moment,
but you have disappeared
and I am left with new growth.

Violets

It was the smell of violets,
the sweet smell of violets,
cut down and bound up
in the house I used to live in.

Pruned with pinking shears,
housed in that tiny room,
the sweet, sickly perfume
making me gag.

It was always violets.
Shades between purple and blue
appearing every Sunday,
colour of a thousand cracked molluscs –
a reminder of humility, of penance.

Scalloped leaves with sharp borders,
jagged edges of repentance,
left to die in water
a lucky penny at the bottom –
but where she left me,
violets grew.

Penelope and Odysseus

Planes are small
against grey and blooming clouds
carrying the journeying dream of man –
a slow drift of distance.

This Sunday of rootless wandering
sings overhead
as I weave shrouds from the air
waiting for your quest to end –
patient like poems that idle inside
for a great length of time.

Cartographer

He holds it up to the light,
this map drawn with pen and ink,
marking where his hands
have crossed the distance.

A paracosm, depicted in detail,
he mimics elevations
traced through exploration
with fidelity to the physicality
of the landscape.

Fingertips travel tributaries and springs,
tracing contour lines of collarbones,
rendering memory in monochrome,

his handmade love showing itself
in the dark fire of a new morning
creating legends known only to us.

The Old Master

He frames her with muted foliate –
        etched intricacies, scored with intention,
border the backcloth of azurite reverie.

The carmine of her heart spills into a crimson lake
        washing upon an earth of umber footing –
raw and burnt and gratified

beneath the orpiment sun where he fills apertures
        no other eye could recognise.
Particular attention is paid to layers of skin:

bone black veins and malachite streaks
        bathed in devotion, in shades that dominate
his palette like the vermilion of her lips

consuming with a timely toxicity –
        breathless and beholden to an art
that will ever be unfinished.

El Corazon

In the seat of your hand lives a flame,
painted to travel the curve of the heart line,
immolating mounts of Jupiter and Saturn.

It radiates with sulphurous incense –
glowing from sincerity to solder my wounds
with curative heat.

Your honest mouth a forge
breathing faith into our universe
with lips that drip gold toward my pharynx.

Press your burning fingers into my skin –
brand me with ruts and hollows we will trace
and fill with tomorrows.

Cast me in the furnace of your artistry
where tenderness unfurls from the flush
of new flesh – divine in its pink reform.

Adorned in your bracelets of fire,
I'll lay swaddled and bound by desire:
El Corazon ablaze.

Pebbles and Bricks

I am light in your hands
though I felt heavy to other men.
I have been made smooth
by way you move me around
the palm of your hand
and the freedom of your water's edge.

Put me in your pocket,
take me home and I will be
the keepsake on your fireplace.
You will fathom mysteries
in the maze of veins that colours
my undulations,
uncovering the splendour

just beneath the surface,
as you stroke your thumb across
my subtle imperfections
time and again.

Nightingale

For D.L

I am a nightingale
in the sky of your longing
raising a garden of sound
across your wild
and febrile landscapes.

I will swallow the sun whole
singing through the night
to lengthen our days
beneath a waxing moon.

Our sonorous communion
will smooth the edges
of boundaries –
the way the tips of your fingers
soften the sharpness
of thorny doubt.

Rise and fall with me
as I wait, uncaged,
for your melody of the morning –
for our vocal tapestry,
clothing this existence
in ribbons of love.

Openhanded

You tell me there's no room for sadness,
flay my grief with the first flood of love
and sustain it with dams built of sinewed devotion.
I cloak the chrysalis of myself in your palm,
an unburdened gift, because my heart is full –
at last, my heart is full.

Previously Published Poems:

'The Unforgiven', *Cape Magazine* (2023)

'Exposure', Rust Chapbook, *Rancid Idols* (2023)

'I Am Not Light', Sound and Vision, *Black Bough Poetry* (2023) (Nominated for Best of the Net)

'Dirt' and 'I Stand Outside Your House and Try to Remember' from 'The Words of Others are All We Have', *Hedgehog Poetry*, (2024)

Pebbles and Bricks, Familial Obligation, Cartographer, *Dreich* (2023)

'1989' and 'Norman Street', *Carmen et Error* (2022)

'House Clearance' and 'Damselflies', *Agenda Broadsheet 23* (2008)

'The Playground', *East Ridge Review* (2024) (Nominated for the Pushcart Prize)

'Strawberries', from 'Afterfeather', *Black Bough Poetry* (2022)

RECOMMENDED READING

Check out these titles from the Bough and friends: The Black Bough Poetry Library (all titles available on Amazon)

Deep Time Vol 1 (Black Bough, 2020)
Deep Time Vol 2 (Black Bough, 2020)
Christmas & Winter Vol 1 (Black Bough, 2020)
Christmas & Winter Vol 2 (Black Bough, 2021)
Dark Confessions (Black Bough, 2021)
Freedom-Rapture (Black Bough, 2021)
Under Photon Crowns, by Dai Fry (Black Bough, 2021)
Nights on the Line, by M.S. Evans (Black Bough 2022)
Sun-Tipped Pillars Of Our Hearts (Black Bough, 2022)
Christmas & Winter Vol 3 (Black Bough, 2022)
Afterfeather (Black Bough, 2022)
Duet of Ghosts (Black Bough, 2022)
Sound and Vision, guest edited by Kitty Donnelly (online only, 2023)
Street Sailing, by Matt Gilbert (Black Bough, 2023)
Tutankhamun Centenary Anthology (Black Bough, 2023)
The Poet Spells Her Name, by Sarah Connor (Black Bough, 2023)
Christmas & Winter Vol 4 (Black Bough, 2023)
In Flight, guest edited by Marcelle Newbold (Black Bough, 2024)
In the Shadow of Gods, by Rachel Deering (Black Bough 2024)
Consolamentum, by James McConachie (Black Bough, 2024)
Christmas & Winter Vol 5 (Black Bough, 2024)
Mountains That See in the Dark, by Regine Ebner (Black Bough, 2025)

Publications by Louise Machen

Pamphlet – The Words of Others are All We Have, by Louise Machen and J. Daniel West (Hedgehog Poetry, 2024)

I Am Not Light, by Louise Machen (Black Bough, 2025)

Publications by Matthew M. C. Smith:

Origin: 21 Poems – Matthew M C Smith (Amazon, 2018)
The Keeper of Aeons – Matthew M C Smith (Broken Spine, 2022)
Pamphlet - Paviland: Ice and Fire (Black Bough Poetry, 2023)

Forthcoming Black Bough Titles

A new anthology, guest edited by Jen Feroze.

Books by Polly Oliver, Helen Laycock, Vikki C, Saraswati Nagpal, Guinevere Clark and more.

T.S. Eliot anthology – TBC

BONUS POEMS

Ritual

I draw my knife across the sharpening stone.
            Back, forth, back.
      Forth, back forth.
Filing dishevelled thoughts with precision –
rhythmic rasps like wings of a moth against the light.
            Back, forth, back.
      Forth, back forth.
Ceremonial strokes of a particular order comfort
uncertainties that loom outside this moment.
            Back, forth, back.
      Forth, back forth.
Every scrape a self-taught catharsis, a reminder
we create our own way of doing things.

Cherry Bakewell for the Fire Gods

Teacups line the garden path like breadcrumbs
signalling refuge of springtime.

A stone table of mismatched kitchen crockery,
eroding from the winter rains,
offers crows' heads on silver trays
tarnished with months of waiting.

We build the fire – pages of sacred books
and kindling broken from beams of a home
we no longer enter.

The cake is made in the way we were taught
and laid on the altar our grandmothers built.
.
Spurs from the flint take hold of crosses
crafted from dried autumn grasses,
igniting tradition that tilts us towards the sun.

Scorpions

"O, full of scorpions is my mind, dear wife." -- Macbeth

The scorpions in my mind
live behind an old green settee
needling at childhood, at naïve beliefs,
in large and pointed dreams.
They travel the weave of fine veins
padding cushions of shame
with vesicles of acute remembering:
predators of opportunity
inebriated by time –
dark and sweet and threatening.

The Condition

It's like walking through a frosted field
at first light – breath visible,
droplets clinging to flesh
exhausted of warmth,
spurred by a search where shadows
stagger and it's not late enough to see.

A paleness of orange leaks
across the petrol-washed sheath of day.
Your feet make shapes in white grass –
the only markers of a pursuit
mapped by an unfamiliar mind.

Only, you're walking in circles –
as dawn grows, the first frost melts
and the green of the ground is an echo
that you are alive,
and she is not.

Harbour

Dreams recede into slumber and darkness
peeling sheets from heavy limbs;
I slip back into his harbour

using the camber of warm skin as my armour,
pulling gently on invisible strings.
Dreams recede into slumber and darkness

echoing the distress of departure –
breath in thick air ripples and sings.
I slip back into his harbour;

a reverie of roses crosses an arbour
appearing distinctly where consciousness thins.
These dreams recede into slumber and darkness

as my need for him spins a harness
of tightly wound forearms and shins
and I slip back into his harbour

weaving red roses through our garden
where a search for lips and arches begins –
dreams recede into slumber and darkness
as I slip back, always, into his harbour.

Misted

The morning-shroud of autumn
confuses details of the dawn.
A cloud of tiny droplets
poised beyond the curtain,
swathes night over streetscapes:
gestation of the shortest day.
I slip back into pillow-thoughts –
this aging house, struggling
with the silence of summer.

Daybreak

A tiny bird, relentless in song,
pierces the day –
her high-pitched aural flare calling:
Find me. I'm here, waiting.

Printed in Great Britain
by Amazon